The Seven Fires
An Ojibway Prophecy

Related by
Sally Gaikesheyongai
art by
Polly Keeshig-Tobias

This book was produced by the collective effort of
The Turtle Island Publication Group and Sister Vision Press

Canadian Cataloguing in Publication Data
Gaikesheyongai, Sally
Seven Fires: An Ojibway prophecy
ISBN 0-920813-92-5

1.Ojibwa Indians – Religion and mythology – Juvenile literature.
2. Prophecies – Juvenile literature. I. Keeshig-Tobias, Polly, 1973 -
II. Title
E99.C6G3   1993   j299'.75   C94-930223-6

Published with the kind asistance of the
Canada Council and the Ontario Arts Council

Published by
Sister Vision Press
P.O. Box 217
Station E, Toronto
Ontario, Canada
M6H 4E2

THE FIRST PROPHECY TALKS ABOUT THE RISING of the Sacred Shell. To me, it speaks of the time before colonialism. The people had a way of life that was based on sacred teachings and they lived out what they thought were the Original Instructions given to them. Those teachings of the Sacred Shell gave them a perspective of themselves – their families, their communities, the whole race, the human family – and they were able to see that we were not the only family on earth.

There was also the plant family, the animal family, and the minerals and resources family. They were able to see that there was not only the world that we could see with our eyes, but there was, as well, a spiritual side to all of life and that there was a Creator who was powerful enough to do all of this.

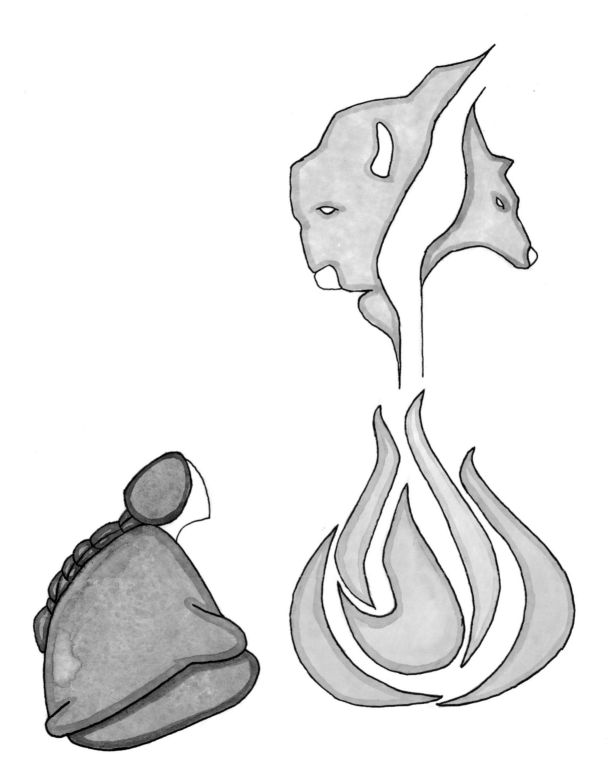

In order to be appreciative of all of that, we had to learn to live in a certain way; we had to learn to live in harmony with all life forms. That feeling – to want to live in harmony – guided them in their community life, their way of governing, and their way of organizing their communities.

They had a very well-rounded education under that system. They had their own health and welfare system because they really looked after each other. They had their own legal system and their own way of governing themselves. They did that for thousands of years because every year they kept reaffirming the Original Instructions they had been given. It's in the time of the First Fire that this way of life began and the people lived a certain way.

THE SECOND FIRE TELLS ABOUT A WEAKENING of the ways. The only way I personally can think of that weakening is to relate it to a human relationship. During the early part of any relationship, both parties see each other in a certain way. In the interest of building a strong bond that will last, each person tends to focus on the good they see in each other and do whatever it takes to bring out the best in each other. They agree to invest in those ways of thinking and doing that will increase the chances of harmony and survival of the relationship. That is how the people were when the Sacred Shell came to them. They welcomed the teachings that would help them to see everything around them as being sacred because their survival depended on the establishing of a way of life that was harmonious, not destructive, to everything they depended on.

Then as happens with everything in life – changes took place. It's only natural in human relationships as well. I think that's what happened to my people. They started changing. They started asking questions about themselves, where they lived, how they lived and why. Perhaps they thought of different possibilities. It happens in all relationships.

As with all change, two kinds of things began to happen: the deterioration of something and in its place, the development of something else. Perhaps a younger generation began to wonder if life might be better if some things were changed somehow. A new vision emerged that stirred the people to move with the change, and some actually began moving to a new place.

T HE THIRD FIRE TALKS ABOUT A MIGRATION OF THE people. Again, I go back to a human relationship. Sometimes we humans need to get away from each other for a while and re-evaluate what the relationship means. We need to question if it really means something to us and determine what is really important in it for us. Sometimes we need the space to go away for a while to do this work. I think the people needed to do that.

Some of them decided that they would move. The Ojibway Nation began migrating eastward. Some groups headed along the waterways to the Manitoulin Island area. Some teachers said that this was where the Sacred Shell wanted the people to move in order to keep themselves and their teachings alive. These people became the Keepers of the Faith, the Keepers of the Fire. A prophecy revealed that they would survive if they moved to that new location. The Original Instructions and Way of Life could not be allowed to die completely, so some of the Ojibway began to make the trek westward.

THE FOURTH FIRE WARNED THE PEOPLE OF THE coming of another race and that good or bad would come of that. It depended on whether or not the members of the other races – the brothers and sisters they had heard about but had never met – remembered their Original Instructions and were prepared to share in a good way all that they had learned about life so far.

I think about the people moving from one area of the country to another. In a sense, they were meeting new brothers and sisters even by doing that. In moving to a new area, they were also meeting new animal sisters and brothers, new plant sisters and brothers, and new minerals and resources which they didn't know about yet. The people didn't know how each was helpful or harmful to their survival. A period of adjustment was needed to re-orient ourselves to how best to live in harmony with these new brothers or sisters.

So this is what has long since happened with the coming of new brothers and sisters from across the ocean. Our philosophy taught us to live in harmony with all that we saw around us, and because we believe in the sacredness of creation, we extended that same feeling towards those people who arrived. We were told about their coming here some day to be among us. We were to be very careful and watch to see if the hand they extended to us carried any weapons or if it was the hand of friendship they extended. Perhaps they were ready to share life with us and perhaps not. Time alone would tell. Time would reveal the truth behind the mask they wore.

A FIFTH FIRE WAS LIT WHEN IT BECAME APPARENT that our new brothers and sisters had forgotten the "sacredness of all things". The Ojibway who, for years, had been able to keep up the cycle of their own traditions and way of life, met up with brothers and sisters who came from a different way of life. They came from a hierarchy system that was a classist system. If you wanted to be a "somebody", you had to climb up a "ladder of success". Those who came, saw all the resources that were here and they started to think in terms of the dollar. They came over here and decided they were going to colonize this land. They were going to get control of everything and claim all this for the greater glory of their king or what they perceived as their "God".

In order to do all this, the newcomers decided they would come up with a system of controlling the people who were already here by way of the Indian Act. The colonizers began to create "Canada" on this soil. However, before they even began creating the tree or system that is Canada, they brought the seeds of sexism,

classism, and racism and planted them as the roots and these seeds helped to shape the branches or systems of control. For example, they have built an education system and a legal system and used their religion to justify the way they oppress and the reason they oppress. This is how and where Canada's Public Institutions originated. All the people who were born on this land are the leaves on that tree. They want us all to become "Canadians". The residential school system was a method of forcing Aboriginal people to "fit in" to a new way of life. They legally tore families and communities apart to make them *fit* into the new country they were building.

Much of the residential school system experience points out that it was not about getting an education. It was about forcing people to assimilate into Canadian Society. It was about wiping out Aboriginal identity. The message underlined to Aboriginal families and communities and whole First Nations was that, in order to survive in this new country, we were to keep silent about being native! Become invisible! Blend in! Assimilate...or else!

T HE SIXTH FIRE TALKS ABOUT HOW THIS WHOLE experience resulted in most Ojibway withdrawing from their cultural, traditional and spiritual values and practices. The Fire that they were to have kept alive almost died during this period.

What saved the Ojibway and their Fire from dying out completely was that enough Ojibway took a great risk. Rather than sending their children to the new "way of teaching", they would instead hide and keep their children with them. Groups of people went "underground". Among them were Ojibway Elders who kept the traditional teachings, values and practices alive. In spite of what was going on around them, they kept the Fire going – that was their ceremonies, their medicines, their drums, their songs, their dances, their language and their stories. They kept the Fire going and waited for the day when others would seek its flames again. They watched for signals that would let them know that the next fire – the Seventh Fire – had been lit and another change was to begin. Some "fell asleep" waiting.

THE SEVENTH FIRE IS THE TIME WE ARE LIVING NOW. It was foretold that in the Seventh Fire, a new people would emerge, a new generation who would not let all the pain and anger and lies stop them from finding out the truth about who they are and what has happened.

It would be a time when the new people would look back over the Trail of Tears of so many generations and ask "why". In looking back, they would notice things others had left beside the trail and they would go back and pick them up and bring those things with them into where we are now. The things that were left behind were the various ceremonies, the medicines, the drums, the songs, the dances, the languages, the stories – all those things that gave meaning to being an Ojibway.

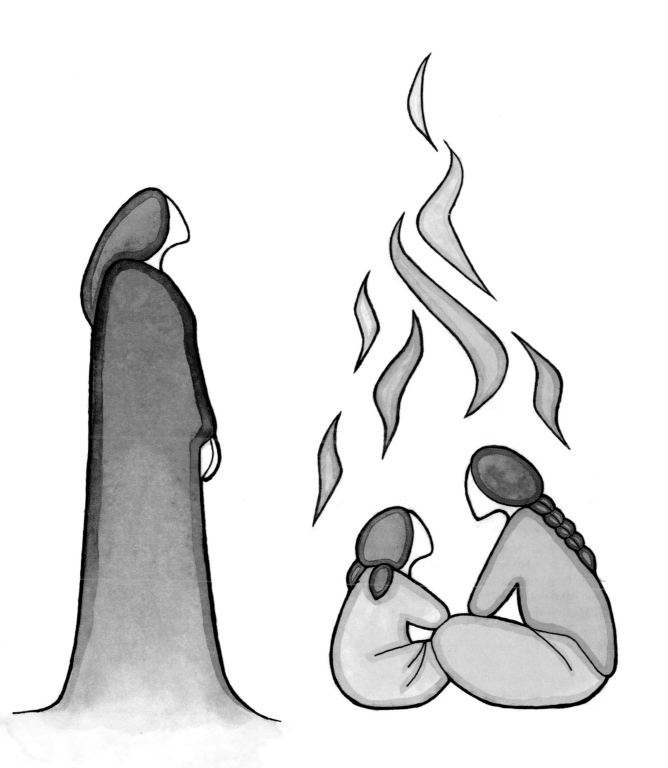

In trying to find the Original Meaning of these things, the new generation had to seek out and find the remaining Teachers and Elders who had this knowledge. They had to find those who had not "fallen asleep". In finding and reclaiming meaning for themselves and their lives, it becomes their task to stir the remaining embers of the Original Instructions into a Fire of Healing in order to bring as many others as possible into rebuilding a Sacred Circle of Life. They are the ones who spend their lives stirring others to waken, discover, and reclaim Culture and Spirituality back into the Circle of their lives. They are the ones who inspire others to walk again, the Good Red Road. That choice is before us now.

WHY ALL THIS AT THIS TIME? THERE IS THE HOPE that somehow, together, we would light the Eighth Fire. Ideally, the Eighth Fire would be one of peace and harmony for all – if we choose carefully the road, we, as human beings, would travel from this time forward. All of creation depends on the choice we make now – individually and collectively. So much healing is needed if we are to ensure our individual and collective survival within the Circle of Life of which we are all a part.

That's where I'd like to end the story.